Dr. Archana Datta
Dr. Subhash Chandra Datta
Amitava Datta

The Wonderland ALASKA

BlueRose Publishers

First Published in July 2020

ISBN: 978-93-90223-26-8

BLUEROSE PUBLISHERS
www.bluerosepublishers.com
info@bluerosepublishers.com
+91 8882 898 898

Cover Design:
Mohd Arif

Typographic Design:
Tanya Raj Upadhyay

Distributed by: BlueRose, Amazon, Flipkart, Shopclues

Preface

People when announce they are going to Alaska the first question they are to face – "Why"? In respect of the location of Alaska the 49th State of the USA has rightly earned its introduction as the" Last Frontier". Location of the last land point on the earth, heavenly atmosphere packed with towering mountains equipped with glaciers and snow peaks, icebergs, its wildlife and wilderness, its indigenous people with Unique lifestyle in harsh climate, work of mother nature in the sky as northern light or Aurora Borealis and so many attractions allure people to visit Alaska.

I, myself, my husband and my son visit Alaska in 2015 in the month of August to September. This book is a travel account. It has been prepared on the basis of personal observations, running commentaries of local guides and web surfing.

I am grateful to my son Amitava Datta who has taken the whole responsibilities of this tour – we have expressed our desire only. I am also thankful to him for providing some valuable photographs and his companion throughout the journey. I am grateful to my husband Dr. Subhash Chandra Datta. This travel account would have been impossible without his tour diary and movie. He supports me in every step of the write up – from framing of the travel account to editing. I am also very much grateful to my grandson Diptopal Das who continuously helps me to handle the computer during my writing and to place the pictures. Thanks are also due to my daughter

Gargi Paul and daughter in law Gargi Mitra (Datta) for their constant inspiration. Last but not the least I should express my gratitude to Dr. Amitava Sarkar, retired Anthropologist of Anthropological Survey of India, who has encouraged me continuously to complete this treatise.

Dr. Archana Datta

Introduction

The name "Alaska" is derived from the Aleut word Alaxsxaq meaning "main land". It is also spelled as Alyeska, literal meaning of which is "the object towards which the action of the sea is directed" (Source: Internet- "History of Alaska" - Wikipedia). The Aluets are indigenous people of the Aleutian Islands. Alaska, the unique vast land has been discovered in 1741, when a Russian expedition team led by Danish navigator Vitus Bering has sighted the Alaskan main land. Alaska has become a Russian colony since 1744 and the name Alaxsxaq or Alyeska as referred by the indigenous people has become "Alaska"to them. United states Secretary, William Seward has offered Russia $7, 2, 00,000 or two cents per acre for Alaska on October 18, 1867. Alaska officially has become the property of the United States. Many Americans have used to call the purchase deal as "Seward's folly". Alaska has become the 49th state of the USA on January 3, 1959.

Location and Geography:

It is the northern and western most state of the USA. Alaska is extended from 54°40' N to 71°50'N latitudes and 130°W to173°E longitudes (approx.). Nearly one third of Alaska lies beyond the Arctic Circle. The Arctic and Antarctic Circles are very important on Earth's map. The Arctic Circle is at 66°30' north of the Equator. This imaginary circle is the southernmost latitude in the Northern Hemisphere where the sun remains above the horizon for 24 hours once per year in summer (in June) and below the horizon for 24 hours once per year in winter (December). This is also true in the Antarctic region of Southern Hemisphere where the Antarctic Circle lies at 66°30' south of the Equator. The state is bordered by Yukon and British Columbia in Canada to the east, the Gulf of Alaska and the Pacific Ocean to the south and south west, the Bering Sea, Bering Strait and the Chukchi Sea to the west and the Arctic Ocean to the north. Total area of the state is 1,717,856 km². It is the largest state of the USA with the lowest density. Total estimated population in 2015 is 738,432 and density of population is 0.43/km² (Source: Internet – "Alaska"- Wikipedia). Alaska is the seventh largest sub national division in the world. It has nearly 55,000 km of tidal shoreline.

Alaska has three important mountain ranges–Brooks Range, Alaska Range and Aleutian Range. Those mountain ranges give Alaska a rugged and beautiful terrain across its entire expanse. Brooks Range is located in the northern North America stretching some 1,100 km from the Chukchi Sea to Canada's Yukon Territory. Alaska Range is relatively a narrow mountain range of Alaska, extending from Lake Clark at its southwest end to the White River in Canada's Yukon Territory in the southeast. Aleutian Range is located in southwest Alaska. It extends from Chakachamna Lake (130 km south west of Anchorage) to Unimak Island, which is situated on the tip of the Aleutian Peninsula. Aleutian Range is special for its large number of active volcanoes. McKinley is the highest peak of North America. Those mountain ranges are characterised by glaciers, earthquakes and continuous volcanic activities. Structurally, the ranges are northwest ward continuation of the Rocky Mountains and Pacific mountain system of North America. Alaska's mountains contain large mineral resources.

Regions of Alaska:

There are no officially defined boundaries demarcating various regions of Alaska. But one can divide Alaska into five regions: (1) Far North, (2) Interior, (3) Southcentral, (4) Southeast and (5) Southwest.

Far North Alaska:

Arctic Alaska or Far North Alaska is a region of the state of Alaska generally referring to northern areas on or close to the Arctic Ocean. It commonly includes North Slope Borough, Northwest Arctic Borough, Nome Census Area and sometimes includes parts of the Yukon – Koyukuk Census Area. The ecosystem is largely of Tundra type covering mountain ranges and Coastal Plains. Brooks Range is a mountain range in Far North Alaska of North America. In the United States, Brooks Range is considered as an extension of the Rocky Mountains. The North coast has been defined as the Arctic Coastal Tundra eco-region. Arctic Alaska is also the home of wildlife refuge, Gates of the Arctic National Park and the National Petroleum Reserve of Alaska. This region experiences the Midnight Sun in the summer and Polar night in winter (Source: Internet - "Arctic Alaska" – Wikipedia).

Interior Alaska:

This is the central region of Alaska, roughly bounded by Alaska Range in the south and Brooks Range in the north. So many mountains are found in this region.

Denali Mts. of Alaska Range is the main tourist attraction of the area. Existence of Denali National Park and Preserve is the great attraction of wilderness. Total area of this region has an estimated population of 113,154. The largest city in the Interior is Fairbanks, Alaska's second largest city (sometimes third also) by population, in the Tanana Valley. It may be said that the vast majority of indigenous native people of Interior Alaska are Athabaskan Indians.

Interior Alaska experiences extreme seasonal temperature variations. Average winter temperature in Fairbanks is -24° c and average summer temperature is +17° c. Both the highest and the lowest temperature records of the state are found in Interior Alaska, with 38° c in Fort Yukon and - 64° c in Prospect Creek. During winter nights, the Aurora Borealis can often be seen dancing in the sky. Fairbanks receives 21 hour of day light between May10 and August 2 in summer and an average of less than 4 hours of daylight between November 18 and January 24 in winter. The interior Alaska is largely underlain by discontinuous permafrost which gradually leads to continuous permafrost as the Arctic Circle approaches (Source: Internet – "Interior Alaska" – Wikipedia).

Southcentral Alaska:

This region consists of the shorelines and uplands of central Gulf of Alaska. The region includes Cook Inlet, the Matanuska-Susitna valley, the Kenai Peninsula, Prince Willium Sound, and the Copper River Valley. The terrain of Southcentral Alaska consists of six mountain ranges – Alaska Range, Talkeetna, Wrangell, Chugach,

Kenai, Tordrillo, and part of Aleutian Range. Southcentral Alaska contains several dormant and active volcanoes. The Wrangell Volcanoes are old, lie in the east. The climate of southcentral Alaska is subarctic. The coastal areas are characterised by temperate rain forests and alder shrub lands. The interior areas are covered by boreal forests. Total population of Southcentral Alaska is about 452,526. The main city of this region is Anchorage. It is the first ranking populated city in Alaska State as a whole. Total estimated population of Anchorage is about 291,538 in 2018. Anchorage is located at the terminus of the Cook Inlet, on a peninsula formed by the Knik Arm to the north and the Turnagain Arm to the south (Source : Internet – "Anchorage, Alaska" – Wikipedia).

Tourism, fisheries, and petroleum production are important economic activities. The city has long been known as "Alaska's biggest native village." According to the 2010 census Anchorage has Native American population of 23,130 (Source Internet: Author: Mike Dunham, 2011 – "Anchorage is Alaska's biggest Native 'Village', census shows").

Southeast Alaska:

Southeast Alaska is locally known as the Alaskan Panhandle or Alaska Panhandle. The region is bordered to the east by the northern half of the Canadian province of British Columbia. The Majority of this region is part of the Tongas National Forest, the United States' largest national forest. The Southeast Alaska or Alaska Panhandle is dominated by Coast Mountains of pacific Coast Range. The range includes volcanic and nonvolcanic mountains and the extensive icefields of the Pacific and Boundary Ranges (Source: Internet: "Coast Mountains" - Wikipedia). Southeast Alaska is noted for its maritime climate means cool summer and mild winter. It belongs to temperate rain forest within the Pacific temperate rain forest zone. Juneau is the largest city of the region and is the capital of the state. Hyder, the eastern most town of Alaska, is also situated in this region. According to 2010 census, Southeast Alaska has been inhabited by 71,616 persons, about 45 per cent of whom are concentrated in Juneau. Now, it is an important route for Alaska Marine Highway ferries as well as cruise ships. The region is also referred as "Inside Passage" (Source: Internet – "Southeast Alaska" – Wikipedia").

Southwest Alaska:

The region includes a huge, complex and relatively unknown terrains. The area is not exactly defined by any Government administrations nor does it always has a clear geographic boundary. It includes a big area that does not have a good number of people or any mentionable urban area. Although much of the area is coastal, it also includes a large area of boreal forests, swamps and highlands and the immense mountain barrier of southern Alaska/ Aleution Range. Aleutian Range is a part of the ring of fire, which means it is on the coast of the Pacific Ocean and has a lot of volcanoes. Southwest Alaska consists roughly of Aleutian Islands, Bristol Bay, Kodiak Island, Lake and Peninsula boroughs, the portion of the Kenai Peninsula Borough that lies west of Cook Inlet; along with Aleutians West, Bethel,

Dillingham and Kusilvak census areas. The region has a combined area of 442,190 km² and total population is about 53349 persons in 2000 (Source: Internet – "Southwest Alaska" – Wikipedia).

Indigenous People of Alaska:

Alaska's Indigenous people are jointly called Alaska Natives/ Indians. Total estimated population of Alaska is 7, 37,438 persons (2018), of which more than 15 per cent belongs to Alaska Natives. They can be divided into five major groups : Aleuts, Inupiat - Northern Eskimos, Yuit - Southern Eskimos, Athabaskans - Interior Indians, and Tlingit and Haida - South east Coastal Indians (Source: Internet – "Alaska Native Communities on Harriman's Route" – PBS).

Aleuts: these indigenous people of Aleutian Islands are found mostly in Southwest Alaska. According to 2000 census, 11,941 people are identified as Aleut (Source: Internet – "Aleut"-- Wikipedia).

Inupiat: traditional territory of this community is in the Arctic Region or Far North from Norton Sound on the Bering Sea to the northern most part of the Canada – USA border. Their total population is about 26,000 in 2010 (Source: Internet – "The Alaska Native Population is on Upward Trend" by Mike Mason – KDLG).

Yuit: as these people speak in Yupik language they are also known as Yupik. They are the most diverse group of Alaskan natives. At the time of contact, they were the most numerous of the Alaska native groups. They are found from Prince Willium Sound on the North Pacific coast to St. Lawrence Island in the central Bering Sea.

They are usually divided into Bering Sea groups and Pacific groups (Source: Internet -- "Alaska Native Communities on Harriman's Route" -- PBS). Their total population is about 34,000 in 2010.

Athabaskans: they live in the Interior Alaska and have to adjust themselves with some of the harshest environmental conditions of the world. They have about 16.6 thousand population in 2010 (Source: Internet – "The Alaska Native Population is on Upward Trend" by Mike Mason – KDLG).

Tlingit and Haida: these communities occupy the islands and main lands of Southeast Alaska. They have over 13,000 population in 2010 (Source: Internet –"The Alaska Native Population is on Upward Trend" by Mike Mason – KDLG).

Wildlife:

Alaska is the home of more than 70 species of mammals, the largest population of bald eagles, the highest concentration of brown bears in the world. Alaska is the last frontier for animals as well as people. Some of the animals that live in Alaska include orcas, humpback whales, mountain goats, moose, caribou, bison, black bears, dall sheep, brown bears, polar bears, etc. Alaskan wildlife is quite varied and thus alluring to nature lovers worldwide.

Alaska's wonderful rugged natural beauty, its vast landscape with pristine wilderness and rich history of native people, its wild life as well as the dance of the Northern Lights have attracted us to visit Alaska. But we could not go to the Southwest Alaska region.

A Few Days In Alaska

We start on the 28th August, 2015 from Charllote International Airport for Alaska and reach Anchorage at 7:30 p.m. (local time of Anchorage) with a transfer at O' Hare Airport of Chicago (transfer time is 40 minutes). Total Flying time between Chicago and Anchorage is about 6hrs. 40 minutes. We go to the Hampton Inn with the shuttle bus of the hotel. It is a chain hotel, located at 4301 Credit Union Drive. After check in, go to the restaurant Glacier Brew House with the hotel shuttle bus up to the visitor's centre in the down town. We have to walk for five minutes to reach the restaurant. After taking dinner, we come out from the restaurant to hire a taxi. Since, it is over 10 p.m. we can not avail of any shuttle bus of the hotel to return. As the time difference between Charlotte and Anchorage is about 8 hours, all of us feel very much sleepy. Coming back to the hotel try to take bed as soon as possible.

It may be noted here that Anchorage is Alaska's most populous city and contains more than 40 per cent of the State's total population. The municipality has an area of 5079.2 km², of which 4395.8 km² is land and 683.4 km² is water. Density of population of Anchorage is about 68/km². It is located in the Southcentral region of Alaska at the terminus of the Cook Inlet at 61°13'N latitude and149°51' W longitude. The city is on a strip of coastal lowland and extends up to the lower Alpine slopes of the Chugach Mountains. Turnagain Arm, to the south, is a fjord that has some of the world's highest tides. Knick

Arm is another tidal inlet (Source: Internet – "Anchorage, Alaska" – Wikipedia).

Kenai Fjord National Park Tour:

On the next day, that is the 29th we get up very early in the morning to get the train for going to Seward. The shuttle bus of the hotel takes us up to the Anchorage railway station at 411, West First Avenue. The train starts at 6:30 a.m. The name of the train is Coastal Classic Train. It has two types of service, one is Gold Star Service and another is Adventure Class Service. The train runs daily from mid May to mid September. As passengers of Gold Star Service we are given golden star emblems. Gold Star Service class is the Alaska Railroad's premium class service. The car itself is very much attractive. It offers passengers glass dome ceilings to allow panoramic views as Alaska unfolds along the tracks and an outdoor upper- level viewing platform- the only of its kind in the world – offers fresh air and an excellent vantage point for photography. On the lower level of the Gold Star rail cars, passengers enjoy a full service dining room. Tickets include meals, all soft beverages and two complementary adult beverages over 21 years of age.

We get comfortable forward facing seats. Alaskan tour guide is providing narration. As we do not have any time for breakfast, feel very hungry. In the meantime complimentary breakfast is served. We take soft drink also. The train is running first through Anchorage residential neighbourhoods and commercial areas. About more than 80 kilometres section between Anchorage and the old Portarage Station hugs the coast line of Cook Inlet and Turnagain Arm. Here we enjoy the awe-inspiring landscape with the steep mountains of Chugach Range plunged directly into the sea, lush stands of alder and spruce nourished by coastal rains and high sun, Beluga whale playing in the sea. Dall sheep and bald eagle are also common (but we do not have the chance to see them). The train slows down for good photo opportunities. People try to take photographs from different parts of the train. Following a brief stop at Girdwood the train enters into the Kenai Mountains, a dramatic landscape of corrugated peaks. The train stays in the mountains mostly away from the roads. Heading up into the mountains we view glaciers, waterfalls, lakes, snowy mountain tops of Chugach Range. We reach Seward at about 11 a.m. The train halts on the shore of Resurrection Bay before making the return journey at 6 p.m. that evening.

We reach Seaward port by a shuttle bus provided by Tour Company keeping our luggage with Kenai Fjord Tour operator. We embark the ship for "Kenai Fjord National Park Tour". Kenai Fjord National Park has been established in 1980 by the Alaska National Interest Lands Conservation Act. The park covers an area of about 2,711.3 km² on the Kenai Peninsula in Southcentral Alaska, near the town of Seward. The park is so named for the existence of numerous fjords carved by glaciers moving down the mountains from the icefield. Snow and ice cover 60 per cent of the park. The Harding icefield, one of the largest icefield in the United States is located in the Kenai Mountains of the Kenai Peninsula of Alaska. It is also partially located in Kenai Fjords National Park. The icefield is the source of at least 38 glaciers (Source: Internet- "Kenai Fjord National Park" –

Wikipedia). The Alaska almanac estimates that Alaska has 100,000 glaciers. The Park lies just to the west of Seward, a cruise ship port. It may be mentioned that the park protects the icefield, a narrow fringe of forested land between the mountains and the sea, and the deeply indented coastline.

 The ship is a 29 metre long non- smoking cruise vessel designed with comfort in mind. Captured views of jagged icy cliffs along the Kenai Peninsula, fjords and calving glaciers – from inside the warm and spacious cabin equipped with seating arrangements and large picture windows or from the multi level observation decks. The ship begins to move slowly at 11:30 a.m. The ship captain starts to narrate; sharing some knowledge of the Seward area's history and terrain. Seward is located on Resurrection Bay, a fjord of the Gulf of Alaska in the Kenai Peninsula. The city is so named after the former Secretary of State Willium H. Seward. It is the southern terminus of the Alaska Rail Road. The captain attracts tourists' attention to a group of sea lions taking rest on the mountain slope or on a small rocky island. In this cruise we enjoy the sight of active tide water glaciers. Suddenly we hear a sound like the crack of a gunshot and watch that a huge chunk of ice block is coming down and falls hundreds of feet down into ocean below. We view otters and groups of whale are playing in the water. The Captain takes the ship near to a big glacier which is coming down straight to the sea and is standing like a wall. It is known as Aialik Glacier. It is the largest glacier in Aialik Bay, located in Kenai Fjord National Park. We replenish our knowledge of geography by seeing lateral moraine and medial moraine as well as floating ice (small iceberg). In this journey we have a complementary lunch. The tour ends at 5:30 p.m. We rent a car from Hertz and reach Cooper Landing. Cooper Landing is a census designated place in Kenai Peninsula, about 160 km south of Anchorage, located at the confluence of the Kenai River and the Kenai Lake. The town is first settled in the 19th century by gold prospectors. It is named after Joseph Cooper, a miner who has discovered gold there in 1884 (Source: Internet - "Cooper Landing, Alaska" - Wikipedia). Its scenic wilderness location attracts tourists. It takes about 57 minutes to reach Kenai Princess Wilderness Lodge at 17245 Frontier Circle. The lodge is situated in a forest area. Cottages, office and the restaurant are all of wooden structure with ethnic touch. The name of the restaurant is Eagle Crest. We take our dinner there.

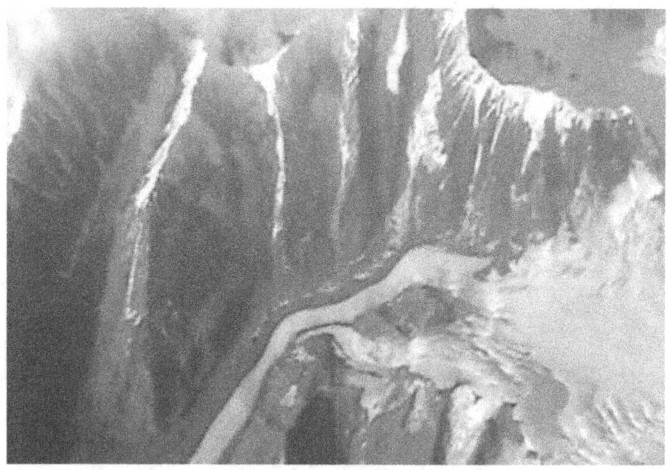

View from the sky

View from the sky

Sunrise from the sky

Gold Star Coach of Coastal Classic Train

View from the train

View from the train

View from the train

View from the train

View from the train

Sea lion

Sea lion

Otter

Whales

Aialik Glacier

Medial and lateral moraines

View of floating ice and sign of glacial calving

View of lateral and medial moraines

Kenai River Canyon Trip:

August 30, the second day of the tour has been fixed for river rafting in the Kenai River; it is being named as "Kenai River Canyon Trip." The Kenai River is a melt water river. The Kenai Lake is its source of origin. The lake narrows to form the river near Cooper Landing. About 19 km from the lake, the river passes through Kenai Canyon for about 3.2km of fast flowing Whitewater Rapids.Flowing about 27.8 km from the Kenai Lake, the river enters the Skilak Lake. This part of journey of the river is known as "Upper River". From the Skilak Lake downstream to the Sterling Highway Bridge near Soldotna, about 31.4 km is known as "Middle River". From the bridge to the mouth at Cook Inlet, about 34 km, is known as the "Lower River". The Kenai River is most popular recreational fishing destination in Alaska, particularly for king or chinook salmon, rainbow trout and dolly varden. The Kenai River area is the home of moose, bears, and various species of birds. The Alaska Department of Natural Resources manage about 169 km area of the Kenai River and lakes as the Kenai River

Special Management Area. We have to go to the office of the Alaska Rivers Company, near the lodge, for dress up and primary instruction to follow during river rafting. There are many other tourists also. The tour company provides life jacket and shoes. The river rafting starts at 10:30 a.m. We three and one driver cum guide are in the boat. It is very windy and cold and is very difficult to hold camera and overhead hood. The beautiful scenic view of nature is mind-blowing. River current is torrential. Each and every moment we have to feel that we may fall down into the river. But the driver can efficiently control the boat. As the boat enters the canyon, wilderness increases more and more. The guide introduces us with the area. At about 1:00 p.m. all boats of this tour company anchor at a river side place. All tourists get down and take complementary lunch provided by the company. All boats start again after taking lunch. We observe, people are enjoying fishing in the river, seagulls are on the shore, ducks are swimming and eagles are sitting on the branches of trees. After completion of the tour at 6:00 p.m. we return our life jackets and shoes to the trip organiser. We start with the shuttle bus through Sterling Highway which meets with Seward Highway Number 9. The Highway is running through Chugach National Forest. We reach Cooper Landing and spend the night in the same hotel.

Kenai River Canyon Trip

Canyon

Kenai River Canyon Trip

Kenai River Canyon Trip

View of Chugach National Forest

Fishing

Lunch

Eagle

Mountain scenery

Returning to the hotel

26 Glacier Cruise:

August 31ˢᵗ, the third day of our trip, we get up at 6:00 a.m. Check out and take breakfast at Eagle Crest restaurant. Then we start from Cooper Landing at about 8:50 a.m. with our car. Reach Seward at 9:25 a.m. and return the car to Hertz office. A shuttle car takes us to the bus stand. The bus going to Whittier starts from Seward at 9:45 a.m. and reaches Whittier port by 11:55 a.m. Whittier is located at 93 km southeast of Anchorage, on the north east shore of Kenai peninsula, at the head of Passage Canal and on the west side of Prince Willium Sound. The region is occupied by Whittier which was once a part of the portage route of the Chugach people. It is said that the Chugach people are the first indigenous Alaskans who encounter the Russian explorer Vitus Bering in 1741.Chugach is the name of an Alaska native people live in the Kenai Peninsula and Prince William on the southern coast of Southcentral Region. The Chugach people are Pacific Eskimo people who speak the Chugach dialect of the Alutiq language. Later the passage has been used by Russian and American explorers and by prospecting miners during the gold rush. During World War II, the United States Army has constructed a military facility, complete with port and railroad near Whittier Glacier. Now this port has become a port of Alaska Marine Highway.

We embark on "Klondike Express" ship for a glacier tour. It is known as "26 Glacier Cruise". Klondike Express is the largest, fastest and most luxurious catamaran in Alaska. Catamaran is a type of boat or ship consisting of two hulls joined by a frame. It can be sailed or motor powered. Catamarans are fishing boats. Today the main use of the catamaran is for day sailing and leisure cruises. It accommodates 332 passengers. The vessel has three decks, two of which are covered and have air conditioned and the third deck has a large outdoor viewing area. Complementary tea, coffee and water are available at self service counters on the vessel. The cruise has departed at about 12:30 p.m. Shortly after the cruise has departed, our crew start to serve a complementary hot meal at our reserved seats. This cruise explores over 225 km of Prince Willium Sound situated in Southcentral Region of Alaska. Prince Willium Sound is a sound coming from the Gulf of Alaska on the south coast of the U.S. state of Alaska, located on the east side of Kenai Peninsula. Most of the land surrounding Prince Willium Sound is a part of the Chugach National Forest and it is ringed by steep and glaciated Chugach Mountain. Captain James Cook entered the Sound in 1778, while he traded with the indigenous people of the area. He called the area Sandwich Sound, but the British Admiralty renamed it as Prince William Sound in honour of King George III's third son. The coastline of this area is convoluted with many islands and fjords. From Whittier, we head eastward through Passage Canal to the Egg Rocks, then continue to scenic Esther passage. Beyond Esther Passage, the vessel heads north into College Fjord, a glacier-rich region. Next we cruise to Barry Arm and Surprise Glacier located in Harriman Fjord. At Barry Arm and College Fjord one can see tide water glaciers. The Captain tries to take us up to the front of the glacier, so that passengers can watch ice calving into the sea. Lastly, we see kittiwake bird rookery, where more than 10,000 birds inhabit during summer for laying eggs, fishing and teaching young hatchlings the survival tips they will need before they fly south for the winter. Kittiwakes (kittiwake is a seabird species in the gull family Laridae) are coastal breeding birds ranging in the North Pacific, North Atlantic and Arctic Oceans. This cruise shows three types of glaciers -- 1) tide water glaciers coming down straight into the water. Here, ice calving is a common feature, 2) Piedmont glaciers at the base of a mountain and 3) Alpine or hanging glaciers.We see seagulls are taking rest on icebergs; sea lions are lying on rocks. We have enjoyed the breathtaking scenery of glacier calving i.e. the breaking of ice chunks from the edge of a glacier. One lady having knowledge of glaciology explains the behaviour of glacier. Otters, different types of whales, like orca whale, humpback whale and variety of birds are common in this cruise.

Cruise has ended at 5:30 p.m. Rail boarding area is very close to the cruise ship. Collecting luggage, we embark the Alaska Train at 6:30 p.m. and depart from Whittier at 6:45 p.m. On the way, we watch Beluga whales in the

Portage Lake visible on our left. Reach Alaska Railroad depot of Anchorage on 1st Avenue at 9:15 p.m. We go directly to a restaurant from the station with a taxi which is available by calling Alaska cab. After dinner we again take a taxi and come to the hotel "Holiday Inn Express" at 4411, Spenard Road.

Seward Highway

Whittier port

Esther Passage

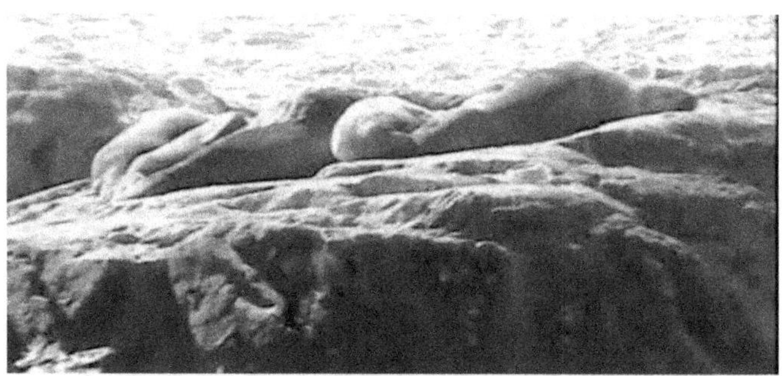

Sea lions

Piedmont Glacier

Hanging glacier

Piedmont glacier

Medial moraine

Tidal glacier

Tidal glacier with ice calving

Seagulls on the iceberg

Waterfalls

Glacial view

Skagway :

On the 1st September, after taking breakfast we go to Anchorage airport with a taxi. Alaska Airlines plane takes off at 7:55 a.m. and reaches Juneau at 9:30 a.m. Juneau is the capital of Alaska located in Southeast Alaska or Alaska Panhandle. Total area of Juneau is 8,430 km² and according to the estimate from the United States Central Bureau, Juneau has a population of more than 32,114 in 2018. The city is named after a gold prospector from Quebec, Joe Juneau. Juneau is unusual among U.S. capitals (except Honolulu, Hawaii) as there are no roads connecting the city with rest of Alaska or with rest of North America (although ferry service is available for cars). The absence of a road network is due to extremely rugged terrain surrounding the city. All goods coming in and going out must avail of plane or boat (Source: Internet -- "Juneau, Alaska" – Wikipedia).

From Juneau we board a plane having ten seats (including the pilot) at 10:30 a.m. and reach Skagway at 11:15 a.m. That is an interesting journey above the lakes, creeks, islands, mountains and glaciers. Then the plane enters a valley to land at Skagway. Skagway is one of the gateways of Klondike Gold Rush. Klondike Gold Rush was a migration between 1896 and 1899 by an estimated 100,000 prospectors to the Klondike region of the Yukon, in north western Canada, east of the Alaskan border, lies around the Klondike River. Most prospectors took the route through the ports of Dyea and Skagway in Southeast Alaska to reach the gold fields. Geographically, it is located at 59°28'7"N and 135°18'21"W, in a narrow glaciated valley at the head of the Taiya inlet. It lies in Alaska Panhandle or Southeast Alaska, 144.84 km northwest of Juneau. According to US Central Bureau, Skagway has a total area of 1200 km², of which 1,170 km² is land and 30 km² is water. It is currently the smallest borough in Alaska (Source: Internet – Skagway, Alaska – Wikipedia). The owner of the hotel takes us to Historic Skagway Inn in Broadway, located towards the end of the main street. It was established in 1897 during the gold rush period as a brothel. It has 10 guest rooms furnished with period antiques. Skagway is a place situated in Alaska where the past lives on through many historic gold rush buildings. Now, the only occupation of the settlers is mostly tourism. Excepting the small planes, tourists can also avail seafaring ships to come and go out of this place. Of course, there are mountain roads to go out of this valley town. Canada border is only about 38.62 km. away. Skagway has two National Protected Area : 1) Klondike Gold Rush National Historic Park (part also in Seattle, Washington)-- it is operated by the National Park Service that seeks to commemorate the Klondike Gold Rush of the late 1890s and 2) Tongass National Forest, the largest national forest in the USA, is managed by the United States Forest Service.

Keeping luggage in the hotel we come to the Rail Road Depot to avail of the train. There are open air exhibitions of Ice cutting machine and the old model of rail engine. We take the train, named "White Pass Express", to get "White Pass Summit Excursion". White Pass and Yukon Railway Route has been built during the Klondike Gold Rush of the late 1890s. White Pass is a mountain pass through the Boundary Ranges of the Coastal Mountains on the border of Alaska and the province of British Columbia, Canada. The Gold prospectors took the White Pass Trail to reach the Klondike region. This trail was narrow, clogged and slippery with mud; many animals became stuck and died. It is estimated that about 3000 horses died on this trail. So, the trail is also known as "the Dead Horse Trail". White Pass Summit was named after Canadian Minister of the Interior, Thomus White in 1887. The train starts at 4:30 p.m. to go to White Pass. This narrow gauge rail road is an international Historic civil engineering. The train runs through the famous land marks such as Bridal Veil Falls - - a long, steep cascade on an unnamed tributary of the Skagway River, the Gold Rush Cemetery located at the north end of the town, and original Klondike Trail of 1898 worn into the rocks. This twenty miles trip -- the Skagway White Pass Excursion climbs from tidewater at Skagway to the summit of the White Pass having an elevation of 873 metres. One can enjoy a breath taking panorama of mountains, glaciers, gorges, waterfalls, trestles and tunnels and historic sites along the White Pass railroad which was used by the prospectors during the Klondike Gold Rush. Every passenger enjoys the unforgettable natural views throughout the fully narrated tour. The train comes back at 8:30 p.m. The place is really very cold. Generally, the climate of Skagway is humid continental type with cool summers and icy winters. Summers are cool to warm with a little amount of rain. The days here receive mild sunshine even at the peak of summer in July with an average high temperature of 19.4°C. Winters are cold with temperature below-17.8°C during many nights. On our return we feel that the town is turned into a deserted sleeping ghostly settlement. This is extremely busy and crowded during noon hours. It may be mentioned that the tourist season is from June to September. About 6000 to 10,000 people visit the place daily in the day time in this season and leave the place in the afternoon.

View from the sky

Creeks from the sky

Rivers from the sky

We are in the aircraft

Glacial lake (aerial view)

Skagway cruise ship Dock

White Pass railway station

Open air museum (ice cutting machine and rail engine)

Railway station of Skagway

White Pass Train

Advertisement during Gold Rush era

River alongside of White Pass

Crossing the river

Glacial view from the train

Bridal Veil Falls

Skagway in the morning

Skagway in the afternoon

Building of Gold Rush era

Journey with M.V. Malaspina:

On the 2nd September we get up as early as 7:30 a.m. and take breakfast at 8:30 a.m. In general, Skagway day starts as late as 10 a.m. due to cold weather and the day population is mostly composed of tourists. By 11:00 a.m. we check out. Then by keeping our luggages in charge of the office of the hotel go to visit the town for last. Ultimately, we leave the hotel at 1:45 p.m. by the hotel car and embark the ship M.V. Malaspina. The M.V. Malaspina is named after the Malaspina Glacier, located in the Wrangell - St. Elias National Park and Preserve, the largest piedmont glacier in the world. MV Malaspina serves Upper Lynn Canal, the deepest fjord in North America and one of the deepest and longest in the world. It connects Skagway and Juneau via Haines and this Inside Passage becomes a major route for shipping, cruise ships and ferries. MV Malaspina operates mostly during the summer as a "day boat" in the Upper Lynn Canal, making daily round trips between Juneau and Skagway with a stop at Haines. The ship is designed to carry 450 passengers with 45 four-berth and 26 two-berth cabins, as well as 1 wheel chair accessible cabin. The ship also can carry wheeled cargo. The vessel is also equipped with an observation lounge, a solarium (a room fitted with extensive areas of glass to admit sunlight); a cafeteria style restaurant, a movie lounge and a child play area. The observation lounge also has a very small museum. The ship starts at 3:00 p.m. and reaches Haines at 4:00 p.m. Cars and other automobiles disembark and embark but passengers are fewer in number.

Haines is located in the Northern part of Alaska Panhandle. The ship leaves Haines at 5:00 p.m. and begins to go through creek or fjord having snow capped mountain peaks on both sides. Since we are cabin passengers, luggages are kept with us. View of the outside can be seen through the cabin windows. We enjoy beautiful sunset from the ship at 6:55 p.m., reach Juneau at 9:30 p.m. and come to the hotel Best Western at 9300 Glacier Highway by 10:15 p.m. Since we have taken our dinner in the ship we have no work to do in the hotel except trying to see the Northern light, but it is in vein.

On the ship

Solarium

Our cabin

Museum in the ship

Museum in the ship

Snow covered peaks and glaciers

Haines port

Pre sunset view

Sunset

McCarthy:

Next day, that is the 6th day of our tour, the 3rd September. Get up very early in the morning. After taking breakfast we leave the hotel Best Western at 6:15 a.m with the shuttle bus of the hotel to reach Juneau airport. The plane takes off from Juneau at 7:30 a.m. and reaches Anchorage at about 9:30 a.m. We rent a car from Hertz and start for Chitina at about 11:00 a.m. It is raining. Amitava drives along the Glen Highway and we reach Chitina at about 3:30 p.m. Chitina is a census designated place located on the west bank of the Copper River at its confluence with the Chitina River. Glenn

Highway is the only road access to Anchorage for most of the state (with the exception of the Kenai Peninsula on the Seward Highway). Car is proceeding with mountain range and glacier in front and the Matanuska River on the right side. From Chitina we avail of a four seater plane including pilot (local people called it Air taxi) of Wrangle Mt. Airs shuttle flights which takes us to McCarthy. On the way, moose, mountain goats and bears are seen. The plane is flying mostly over the river valley, frozen rivers, forests, barren mountains, different glacial characters as well as snow capped peaks on the mountain ranges. Reach McCarthy at 4:45 p.m. McCarthy is located in the South Central Region on the foot of the Wrangell Mountains having an area of 384 km² (approx.) with 28 people during the census of 2010 (Source: Internet -- "McCarthy, Alaska" - Wikipedia). From McCarthy Airport we again board on another 6 seater plane including the pilot to have the tour "Grand Flightseeing". It is of 90 minutes tour of "Wrangell Mountain Air". The pilot cum guide of "Wrangell Mountain Air" aircraft shows with narration Wrangell-St. Elias National Park having 53,320.57 km² areas and part of the world's largest preserved wilderness. The park includes a large portion of the Saint Elias Mountains having most of the high peaks in the United States and Canada. The park has been shaped by the competing forces of volcanism and glaciations. Mt Wrangell is an active volcano, one of the several volcanoes in the western Wrangell Mountains. The aircraft has been flying over the snow capped mountains, glacier, glacier with walls that looked like wrinkles, the Matanuska River, barren mountain slope, mountains covered with wild flowers, lateral and medial moraines. Suddenly, total landscape is changed into white colour with the snow covered mountains. It is a very breath taking journey. Our pilot is excellent, very knowledgeable and experienced. The landscape is spectacularly beautiful and the park is absolutely incredible. This is the most amazing experience in terms of beauty, wilderness and solitude. We feel excited when the aircraft is coming down near the snow capped mountains. After completion of this 90 minutes thrilling tour coming down to the ground our feeling is just woke up from the dream. We come to the hotel Ma Johnson by a shuttle van of the hotel at 101, Kennicott Avenue. Keeping luggages we take our dinner at the New Golden Saloon, located very near our hotel. Come back to the hotel.

Glen Highway

Matanuska River (frozen)

Moose

Snow covered mountain ranges with barren Mountain

River valley

Frozen river

Wrangell Mountain Air Taxi with our pilot

Imprint of volcanism and glaciations

View of the mountain

Lateral and medial moraines

Glacial lake

Colourful landscape

McCarthy

Our hotel

Matanuska Glacier:

On the7th day, the 4th September, it is raining continuously from the morning. We take our breakfast at Golden Saloon. Today, we see an Art Gallery named as "Mountain Art". We go to a place from where the shuttle bus uses to pick up the passengers. After a long waiting the bus comes and takes us to the airport. We start from the McCarthy at 9:30 a.m. by a small aircraft that has accommodation for 5 persons including the pilot. Reach Chitina at10:30 a.m. It is still drizzling. On the way, we take a halt at Matanuska-Susitna Park to see Matanuska Glacier. Matanuska Glacier is a valley glacier located at a height of 4,020 m above sea level. The park is located in the Matanuska–Susitna valley surrounded by three mountain ranges – the Alaska Range, the Talkeetna Mountains and the Chugach Mountains. We see 6.5 kilometers wide terminus of the glacier from the Glen Highway on the approach to the Glacier. It is the largest glacier in the United States accessible by car. The Glacier Park itself is a private camp ground which charges a fee to visit the glacier. From there, we have to drive the three kilometer private road and arrive at the beginning of the 20 minute self guided trail. From there we start to walk following the trail marked by orange cones. We have to walk over the ice of the terminal moraines and observe crevasses, hummocky features of terminal moraines, lichen, etc. The path is very slippery so it is difficult to keep balance. We reach the face of the glacier. After this awesome trail tour we have to drive for 5 hours to reach Anchorage and take a halt for the night at Hampton Inn.

Matanuska Glacier

Icy path

Crossing a bridge

Crevasse

Hummocky icy surface with lichens

On the Glacier

Barrow (Utqiagvik):

On the 5th September morning, the 8th day of this tour, we start from Anchorage airport with a plane of Alaska Airlines for Barrow. The plane reaches Deadhorse, the oil town located near the Prudhoe Bay in Far North Region of Alaska and one of the three cities above the Arctic Circle to which Alaska Airlines use to fly; the other two are Kotzebue and Barrow. The flight reaches Deadhorse on time but due to bad weather we have to wait for one and half hours and ultimately reach Wiley Post – Will Rogers Memorial Airport of Barrow at 12:30 p.m. This airport is a 1 building terminal for Alaska airlines only. It is not that impressive, but it serves its purpose for the people who are interested to explore the "Last Frontier". At present Barrow is known as Utqiagvik. This native name refers to a place for gathering wild roots and it comes from the Inupiat word *utqiq* used for potato. This native name is adopted later in 2016.

Mike, the driver of the hotel van, as well as an Inupiat Eskimo, is at airport to pick up us. We reach "Top of The World Hotel" maintained by the tourism department. It is well known for Inupiat Eskimo hospitality. Keeping luggage in the room and taking lunch we go by a van with Mike, the driver cum guide, to have a short visit of Barrow. He gives us a very comprehensive tour, stopping at all important places giving opportunity to take photographs. The name Barrow is derived from Point Barrow and is named after Sir John Barrow of the British Admiralty by explorer Frederick William in 1825. Non-native Alaskans find it easier to pronounce than the Inupiat name. A post established in 1901 helps the name "Barrow" to become dominant (Source: Internet – "Utqiagvik, Alaska" – Wikipedia). Barrow is located in the Far North Region of Alaska at 5 meters above sea level of the Arctic Ocean with geographic coordinates 71°18'N and 156°48'W(approx.). The city has a total area of about 55 km², 47 km²of the area being land and 8 km² water with a total population of about 4500. Owing to its location Barrow's climate is cold and dry, classified as a polar climate. Weather in winter is extremely harsh because of the combination of cold and wind, while summers are cool. The hottest day of the year is mostly on July 26, with an average of 8.33°C and low of 2.22°C. The cold season lasts mostly from November 24 to April 5 with an average daily high temperature below -16.11°C. The coldest day of the year is mostly on January 25 with an average low of -28.33°C and high of -22.22°C. People of Barrow see the sun continuously above or below the horizon for more than one day. Due to its extreme latitude, Barrow experiences polar day (known as midnight sun) during the summer and polar night during the winter. It is overcast year round. Regarding precipitation, Barrow has a cold desert climate with an average rainfall less than only 127 mm per year. Mike shows whaling boat, remnant of a whale, ice cellar, Eskimo dog, jaw of a Bow head Whale. Then the van runs through an unpaved road. On the way we see the technical school. It may be mentioned here that all roads are unpaved due to permafrost. At Barrow, the ground was underlain with continuous permafrost to a depth of around 400 meters. It is observed that a wide area is covered by Lichen. Lichen is considered to be among the oldest living things. Motorable road ends at a place. We have to get down and come to the beach of the Arctic Ocean where it is written in English "Welcome to Barrow" and in Inupiat "Paglagivsigin Utqiagvigmun" framed by whale jaw bones. We come to the Point Barrow. Point Barrow or "Nuvuk" is a headland on the Arctic coast of Alaska. It is the Northern most point of all the territories of the United States. Here we see the northernmost totem pole in the world. Seeing the Arctic Ocean we become excited with a feeling we have reached one of the extreme land points of the Arctic where one side is flat Arctic Tundra and the other side is Ocean which use to remain frozen most of the year. We soak our feet in the chilled cold water. Mike informs that Barrow has satellite access. It is mostly dominated by Inupiat or Inupiaq Eskimo population. It is already said that Eskimos are divided into two groups Yupik and Inupiat.

About the education we come to know that Barrow has Fred Ipalook Elementary School (Prekindergarten to the 5thgrade), Eben Hopson Middle School (6th to 8th grade) and Barrow High School (9th to 12th grade), Ilisagvik

College – a two year tribal college. Barrow has an artificial turf field of Barrow High School football team.

Mike takes us to the Inupiat Heritage Centre. On the rooftop of the world, the Inupiat Heritage Centre in Barrow tells the story of the Inupiat people who have thrived for more than thousands of years. We enjoy taxidermy of birds. The Inupiat Heritage centre is small but really good for understanding whaling and some of the daily activities of the people living above the Arctic Circle. From this Heritage Centre we come to know that women's role in whaling. Women are of integral part for the survival and well-being of Inupiat. Women are keepers of the spiritual, physical, emotional and moral well-being of the captains, their husbands, and the crewmembers. They keep their homes clean before and during whaling. They think that it will help whale to be encouraged to come to their crews. Before hunting women prepare the skin boat, sew new clothing, help all male members to be geared up for whaling and feed them when they go out on the ice. They believe that men may hunt the physical whale; the spirit of the whale gives it to the women. The women maintain the sanctity of the home, feed the needy, and care for others. In early days of whaling, they had proper practices and behaviour dictated by the shaman. Inupiat used to believe that the spirit of the whale was directly tied to their behaviour, especially that of the whaling captain's wife. Women had to follow certain behavioural taboos, such as not sewing during whaling and not speaking improperly. At present, their traditional beliefs are no longer practiced. Now, Inupiat people begin the whaling season with the church service to pray for safety and success. Generally, whale hunting is practiced twice in a year: 1) the spring whale hunting (from early April to first week of June) and 2) the Fall hunting (from early October before the winter begins and continues till the onset of deep darkness). Actually, they have the target in this time to catch whales which must feed the Inupiat families throughout the cold season ahead. They share the hunted whale with everybody and care for the elderly and needy people of their community. Whaling is pivotal point of Inupiat lives. Parched at the edge of the Arctic Ocean, people of Barrow depend on the ocean for their very survival. They survive largely on hunting whales, seals, walrus, waterfowls, polar bears, caribou and catching fish from the Arctic Ocean or nearby rivers and lakes. Subsistence hunting of Bowhead Whales gives the Inupiat culture – strength, confidence and meaning. Inupiat use to teach their children the process of Bowhead Whale hunting at an early stage. Besides that, at present they work in different Government or private services. Tourism also has opened a great source of income for the local people. The Heritage Centre also has craft room where one can see wonderful art work.

If luck favours one can see various birds, whales, seals, Arctic foxes, caribou, brown bears, wolves, beavers and polar bears in Barrow. But we cannot see any of them except a bird named Jaeger also known as Arctic Skua.

Point Barrow is the end of the road of the city. Barrow has no road connection with rest of Alaska. Alaska Airlines with passengers connect Barrow with Anchorage and Fairbank. Multiple Jet air craft, from Deadhorse, Anchorage and Fairbank, provide daily mail, cargo and passenger services. Smaller single and twin-engine general aviation aircraft provide regular service to other villages with Barrow. Barrow is also served by several car services (four-wheel drive vehicles) in and around the city.

Samuel Simmonds Memorial Hospital at Barrow is the northern most hospital/medical facility in the United States. People of Barrow are able to access the hospital by road. However, because no roads lead to or out of the city, individuals in surrounding communities and towns must be airlifted by plane, helicopter, or air ambulance.

Mike showed houses of Eskimos. Eskimo houses are built on pilings on the side of the road. In front of some houses whaling boats are placed. It is said that about 61% of Barrow residents live in single family homes. While about 7% live in mobile homes or trailers. The remaining residents live in buildings with two or more dwelling units. Barrow is among the oldest permanent settlements of the United States. At present the Eskimos do not live in igloos made of dry, hard compacted snow. Ice houses are only built as temporary shelters during winter hunting trips. Permanent houses are usually built of wood, whalebone and covered with seal skins and soil. After 3 hours tour we come back to the hotel.

Wiley post/Will Rogers Memorial Airport

Whaling Boat and remnant of a Whale

Inside the ice cellar

Eskimo dog

Jaw of the Bow head Whale

Unpaved road and Technical Schools

Welcome to Barrow

Arctic Ocean

Point Barrow – the northern most totem pole in the world

Artificial turf field of Barrow High School Football Team

Inupiat Heritage Centre

Eskimo Houses

Denali:

On September 6th, get up early in the morning and enjoy the beauty of endless Arctic Ocean. The "Top of the World Hotel" is situated near the Arctic Ocean beach. So, the ocean can be seen from our room. After breakfast we move to the airport with shuttle van of the hotel. We have to wait at the airport lounge as the air craft cannot land due to bad weather. We come to know that passengers of previous day are also stranded there due to nonavailability of the scheduled flight. Ultimately, a plane named 'Disney' comes after more than one hour waiting and takes all the passengers of two days and flies to Fairbanks. About 40 passengers get down at Fairbanks and another 40 new passengers join us to go to Anchorage. From the airport we go to Hampton Inn by the shuttle van of the hotel. Then after taking shower and lunch we go to the Anchorage airport and take an air taxi at about 6:30 p.m. to reach Kantishna Airstrip. It is an Alaska State owned airstrip, located in Denali National Park and Preserve. During our journey the pilot cum guide narrates character of the landscape below. Shows glacial moraine features. We enjoy snow, snow and snow below. Reach Kantishna Air strip at 8:00 p.m. and see the McKinley Peak (6,190 m). There from the hotel shuttle van picks us to the Kantishna Roadhouse. It is a back country lodge resort in the heart of Denali National Park and Preserve. The Koyukon people of Denali use to refer "Mt McKinley" as "Denali" for centuries. The word "Denali" is used by the native people to mean the "High One" in their language. The Koyukon are an Alaska native Athabaskan people of the Athabaskan speaking ethno linguistic group. In 1896 a gold prospector has officially named "Denali" as "McKinley" in support of the then presidential candidate William McKinley. In August 2015, that name of the mountain is changed to "Denali". It is the highest mountain peak in North America and the third most isolated peak on earth after Mt Everest and Aconcagua (Source : Internet – "Denali" – Wikipedia).

Kantisna Roadhouse has offered an all - inclusive once in a lifetime Alaskan travel experience. It is located in the pristine natural wonder of Denali National Park in a remote area where a few are lucky one to travel. They have bus transportation into the heart of Denali Park, deluxe log cabin accommodations, meals, and a variety of daily activities, hiking opportunities, and chance to observe wildlife and experience the beautiful scenery of the Park. We reach Kantishna Roadhouse at 8:15 p.m. After setting in log cottage No. 27 go for dinner. Dinner has been served in family style. We take fish, smashed potato, corn and black beans with desert of apple cranberry pie topping with cream. After taking dinner we come back to our cottage and see some Japanese girls have gathered at the front of our cottage setting their cameras. Come to know that, they are trying to watch Aurora or the Northern light. We also participate with those girls and see the light partially at about 12:00 o'clock at night.

Next morning, the 7th September, get up as late as 7:00 a.m. After breakfast we go for a hiking in a group along a trail. A lady guide accompanies us. She tries to introduce us with the natural vegetation of the area. We see blue berry, red berry, lingon berry and crow berry bushes. As

Denali National Park is located at north of 61° north latitude there are only a handful of tree species those are able to grow and reproduce naturally in this far north. We can identify spruce and birch only. Bushes are common. There are some medicinal plants. Some bushes are used to work as fertilizer. The guide says, visitors of Denali use to be excited to see "Big Five" – moose, caribou, dall sheep, wolf and grizzly bear. But during this hiking none of us can see any of those animals. We come back to the Kantishna Roadhouse and enjoy the sled dog race. It is demonstrated at 1:00 p.m. One lady delivers a lecture on "Adopt or Die" i.e. environmental adaptation at 3 to 4 p.m. Then we try again to trace wild life along the nature trail but cannot go far as there is a creek on the way and shoes may get wet. Moreover, rain has started, so we have to come back to our cottage. Appetizer is served at 5:00 p.m. and dinner at 6:00 p.m. The weather is not comfortable at all due to occasional rain. During hiking our shoes and socks get wet. The lodge has a place to dry the wet materials. We go there and hand over our shoes and socks to dry and take gumboots. We go to the Moose creek. Gold panning will be demonstrated there. Many tourists have come to participate in the programme. Subhash, Amitava and three other persons have got a sand size gold. It is tiny but a life time memory. Come back to the cottage after returning their gumboots and taking back our socks and shoes. On the way a cache come to the notice. Caches are used to store food to keep out of reach of animals. As it is cloudy there is no scope to see Aurora. Go to bed early.

At Kantishna Airstrip

Kantishna Roadhouse

Our cottage

Blueberry

Redberry

Sled dog race

Gold panning

Cache

Denali and Fort Yukon :

The day of the 8th September starts early. It is quite dark. We have to keep our luggage at our door front before 5:20 a.m. Those will be collected by lodge staff to be kept in the bus. Take breakfast, and have a nice photograph of Denali or McKinley Peak. The bus starts at 6:20 a.m. for a tour. It is still dark and quite cold. We get a clear lucrative view of Alaska Range during our bus journey. The driver cum guide narrates the history of the park. Denali National Park and Preserve is located in Interior Alaska. The park and contiguous preserve encompass 24,464 km². On December 2, 1980 about 8,687km² area of the park has been established as Denali Wilderness. The park is served by the 146.45 km long Denali Park Road. Denali's landscape is a mix of forest at the lowest elevations, including deciduous and taiga, with tundra at middle elevations and glaciers, snow, and bare rock at the highest elevations. The longest glacier of the Alaska Range in the U.S. state of Alaska is the Kahiltna Glacier. The Driver cum guide helps us to see animals. We see bear, moose, caribou and dall sheep. Dall sheep are found in bands on the top or slope of the mountain. Bears are seen near the river or less inclined slope. Moose and caribou are found in the bushes and flat grass lands. We cannot spot wolves throughout the journey but enjoy the natural beauty of Denali National Park and Preserve.

The bus reaches Denali Visitor's Centre at 11:30 a.m. The pickup van takes us from the gate of the Visitor's Centre at about 12:40 p.m. There are three other passengers in the van. We reach Hampton Inn of Fairbanks at 4:30 p.m. The hotel is located at 433 Harold Bentley Avenue. After being fresh and taking dinner we go to the Yukon office at 550 of the 1ˢᵗ Avenue, Fairbanks for a flight at 7:00p.m. to go to Fort Yukon. The original name of Yukon was Gwichyaa Zhee. Gwichyaa means Gwich'in speaking people those who live in the Yukon Flats area of Alaska. The Gwich'in language belongs to Athabaskan language family of Canada and Alaska. Zhee means village in Gwich'in language. Gwich'in Zhee has become the village of Fort Yukon, developed from a fur trading out-post, established by Alexander Hunter Murray of the Hudson's Bay Company. Fort Yukon is located in the north of Arctic Circle at 66°34'2"N and 145°15'23"W at the confluence of the Yukon and the Porcupine rivers. The Yukon River is a major watercourse of north western North America. The source of the river is in British Columbia, Canada. Then it flows through the Canadian Yukon territory and empties into the Bering Sea. The lower half of the river lies in Alaska. It is the largest Athabaskan village of Alaska and one of the oldest settlements in Alaska. Generally, all Athabaskan people (known as Indian to Americans) live along the Yukon River from Canada to Alaska.

Warbelow's flight takes about one hour to reach Fort Yukon. Warbelow's pilot and Richard help us to come down from the plane. Richard the head of Fort Yukon, an Athabaskan, meets us and takes us to a bus of "Alaska Yukon Tours". He is also our guide cum driver. He introduces us with Fort Yukon saying his grandmother came from Canada and grandfather lived in Alaska. Even before hundred years back these people had no modern religion, they were rather animists. The British fathers baptized them and converted them to Christianities. Originally, they used to cremate their dead bodies. But now, dead bodies are buried in a particular burial ground. Christianities gave them many things, now almost all of their people are literate. According to Richard, Fort Yukon has 500 people and most of them are living on subsistence lifestyle relying on fish from the Yukon River and wild animals. On our journey, we see modern houses, well dressed and smart boys and girls and observe that most of the households own four wheeler cars and motorized boats. The Northern light is included in the tour plan, but we cannot see Northern Light due to cloudy weather, but observe very nice sun set in the Yukon River. After completion of this tour all of us get certificates for crossing the Arctic Circle.

Denali or McKinley

Alaska Range

Grizzly bear

Dall sheep

With the pilot and guide

Our guide in front of Fort Yukon Office

We are at Gwichyaa Zhee

Athabaskan settlement

A nice sunset in Yukon River with an Athabaskan child

Alaska Museum and Aurora Borealis:

We spend the morning of the 9th September in Hampton Inn without any work. We enjoy a long leisure time on that day. In the afternoon, we go to the University of Alaska Museum of the North (Fairbanks). It is built recently. Formerly, it was known as the University of Alaska Museum. The museum was shifted at different locations till 1936, when it was housed in Signer's Hall, in Philadelphia, Pennsylvania. Before that, the collections were displayed or stored in several locations around the campus. Over time, the collections overflowed the space. This new building was opened at Fairbanks to the public in late 2005. Wonderful architecture and award winning exhibits make the museum an extraordinary destination to discover Alaska Native culture, natural wonders and diverse wildlife, all in one stop. Museum is not very big but very informative and magnificent exhibits showing actual stuffed animals and information of the way of Alaskan survival. A film about the Northern Lights is shown. After completion of museum visit we come back to the airport by bus. It is interesting to note that there is no bus fare for senior citizens. From the airport we come to the hotel by shuttle van. We go to the forested part near the hotel at about 1:00 a.m. to see Aurora Borealis. Firstly, we observe shooting rays that light up the sky with an eerie glow and are spreading in the northern side of the sky from east to west. Then rays convert to green colour cloud like bands and changes to rippling curtains of green, violet and pink colours.

The word aurora is derived from the name of the Roman Goddess of the dawn Aurora, who travels from east to west announcing the coming of the sun. The Eskimos of Alaska believe that Aurora Borealis are the spirits of the animals they have hunted: the seals, salmons, beluga whales and deer. The bright dancing lights of the aurora are actually collisions between electrically charged particles from the sun that enter the earth's atmosphere. The lights are seen above the magnetic poles of the northern and southern hemispheres. In the Arctic Circle they are known as Aurora Borealis or the Northern Lights and in the Antarctic Circle they are called Aurora Austalis or the Southern Lights. Location of Fairbanks is ideal for viewing Aurora Borealis because it is under the "Auroral Oval", a ring shaped zone over the far north where "aurora" activity is concentrated. Moreover, low precipitation and distance from coastal areas contributes to consistently clear nights. All of these variables make the Fairbanks region an outstanding destination for viewing Aurora Borealis or Northern Lights. Fairbanks' Aurora season is from August 21 to April 21 and the Aurora will be visible here on an average of four out of five nights when the sky remains clear and dark enough. Auroras are best observed around midnight – when the sky remains darkest and on a clear night at a location away from the city, because, deep darkness is essential to view "Aurora Borealis". Anyhow, witnessing of Alaska's "Aurora Borealis" or Northern Lights is an incredible and once-in-a-lifetime experience.

University of Alaska Museum of the North (Fairbanks)

Actual stuffed Grizzly bear

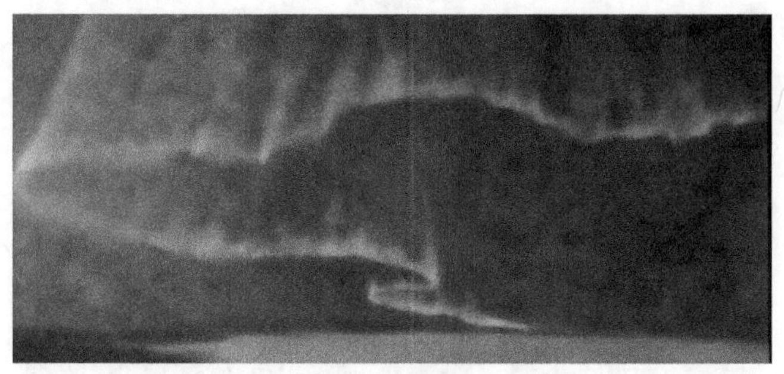

Aurora Borealis

Aurora Borealis

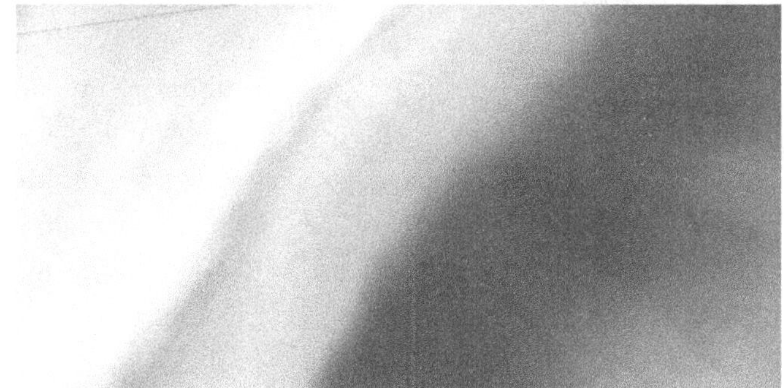

Aurora Borealis

Anaktuvuk Pass:

On the 10th September, we have the programme to spend whole day at Anaktuvuk Pass. Anaktuvuk Pass is named after the Anaktuvuk River. Anaktuvuk is the English way of spelling Annaqtugvik denotes the "place of caribou droppings" in Inupiaq, the language of the Inupiat. There was a nomadic group of Inupiat (Eskimo) called Nunamiut (people of the land) that lived inland in Northern Alaska depending upon hunting caribou. At present, Anaktuvuk Pass is the only Nunamiut settlement in Alaska and a federally recognized Alaskan village. According to the United States Census Bureau, its total land area is 12.4 km² and 0.3km² is water.

We reach the private airport and check in at 8:00 a.m. Our Warbelow's flight starts at 9:00 a.m. It is a 10 seater plane. We are four only. The weather is not good. The pilot is the same who has taken us to Fort Yukon. We reach Coldfoot after 1 hour journey. After reaching Coldfoot the fourth person gets down. Coldfoot airport, on the west side of the Dalton Highway, is an unpaved airport. The plane is carrying goods for Anaktuvuk Pass. Coldfoot has been founded as a gold-mining camp in 1898. Originally, it was a mining camp known as State Creek. The name was changed when many prospectors got "cold feet" upon winter's arrival. Coldfoot is situated at 67°15'N latitude (approx.) and 150°11'W longitude (approx.). The importance of this settlement is the only true truck stop along the highway, and "the world's northern most truck stop".

In the meantime our pilot informs us the plane cannot be able to take us to Anaktuvuk Pass due to bad weather.

We come back to the Warbelow's office and meet with an Eskimo group of Anaktuvuk pass. They are waiting for the flight to return to their home. We come to know from the discussion with a lady teacher of the group that in about 1949 they came on foot from the west to settle here. They are Inupiat Eskimo of Nunamiut clan. Their population is 378. They have one high school including elementary level with 98 students. Their marriageable age is 18 years. Their literacy rate is 100%. Originally, people of Anaktuvuk Pass were nomadic and lived by hunting caribou instead of marine mammals and fish usually hunted by the rest of the Inupiat, who use to live on the coast. Now, they have settled in Anaktuvuk Pass permanently. Generally, they depend on hunting, fishing and gathering. Hunting and trapping for sale of skins, guiding hunters, or making traditional caribou skin masks or clothing provide their sustenance, though some residents have sought seasonal employment outside the town. But, now a day, many people are in white colour job, one of them is a lecturer of a college in mainland, USA. Sale, import and possession of alcohol are banned in the village. Anktuvuk Pass is classified as an isolated area. One health clinic is the only available health care facility for the people of Anaktuvuk Pass. On emergency, people have to avail of air services to go to the city. There are no doctors on site. Auxiliary health care is provided by Anaktuvuk Pass Volunteer Fire Department.

After a long discussion we are called from the office and they give us one certificate each for crossing the Arctic Circle. At last their bus drops us to the hotel. After taking dinner we go out of the hotel to watch Aurora Borealis. But it is not as nice as of previous night.

Cold foot airport

Eskimo group of Anaktuvuk Pass

The end of our tour:

September, 11th, get up as late as 8:0 a.m. After taking shower and breakfast we try to take a nap for one hour more. Then go to the office of North Alaska Tour Company for going to Coldfoot by plane to join the tour "Aurora overnight". Actual flying time is at 1:00 p.m. But the office tells us that the plane will start at 2:00 p.m. At last after 2:30 p.m., the office announces the cancellation of the tour due to inclement weather. We come back to the hotel with a disheartened soul by the bus provided by the tour company.

September 12, the last day of our tour. We get up at about 5:30 a.m. After taking bath and breakfast we start for the Fairbanks railway station to get train for Anchorage. The train starts at 8:15 a.m. from Fairbanks. The driver helps us to get up the train. The name of the train is Denali Star. Denali Star is a passenger and semi luxury train operated by the Alaska Rail Road between the cities of Anchorage and Fairbanks. It is operated between Middle of May and middle of September. It has "Adventure" and "Gold Star" services. We avail of Gold Star service. The train with Gold Star service consists of glass-dome ceilings to allow panoramic views as Alaska unfolds along the tracks, and an upper level outdoor viewing platform for photography. Passengers enjoy a full service dining car on the lower- level of Gold Star rail car. Gold Star passengers enjoy breakfast, lunch and dinner, all soft beverages and two complementary adult beverages for passengers over 21. As Gold Star passenger we take breakfast for second time at 10:00 a.m. and enjoy the iconic landscapes through large windows with narration by Alaskan tour guide. Reach Denali station at 12:10 p.m. and leave by 12:30 p.m. We take lunch at 2:30 p.m. and reach Talkeetna at 4:40p.m. and leave that station at 5:00 p.m. After a small stop at Wasilla from 6:15 to 6:20 p.m. reach Anchorage just at 8:00 p.m. In the meantime we complete our dinner on board. It may be said that about 12 hours train ride covers 563.27 km and is like an expedition, passing through different climates and natural vegetation zones. Many travellers break up trip with stopover at Talkeetna and/or Denali National Park. The route spans two of Alaska's five geographic regions – South Central and Interior Alaska. After getting down from the train we collect our luggage from the trolley of railway department and reach the airport by a taxi. After check in and security clearance we go to the gate number B7 and board on the United Aircraft. After some times our aircraft takes off.

Conclusion

Alaska - "the Last Frontier" of the USA is one of the last unspoiled lands. It is the largest state of the USA and one of the most uninhabited areas in the world. Still it is maintaining its pristine beauty with its wilderness, towering mountains, and snow covered peaks, icebergs, glacial lakes and glaciers. When the last iceage ended, the glaciers retreated to the top of the world as they melted away. At present, they are found in Alaska and Canada's far north as well as Greenland of the northern hemisphere. Alaska is full of glaciers. Sometimes total landscape turns into white colour when one observe Alaska from the sky. It has massive tracts of wild open spaces. Alaska's unspoiled wilderness provides some of the best wildlife habitat for animals. One can observe here some awesome wildlife; it may be whales, moose, bald eagles, bears, caribou or moose. One can enjoy midnight sun in summers and total darkness in winters. To see Northern Light is once- in- a- lifetime experience. Nobody find a better place to witness the full beauty of nature than Alaska. Its natural beauty is incomparable to any other place on earth. We leave Alaska with handful of lifetime memories – mesmerising natural landscape, wilderness of its National Parks, wildlife, and life style of indigenous people and impact of whale on their socio-economic life, experience of touching Arctic Ocean from Barrow – one of the last land points of the earth, divine beauty of Aurora Borealis and so many things. Good bye Alaska.